Marcia Castro Leal

ARCHAEOLOGICAL
MEXICO

220 Colour illustrations

MONCLEM
EDICIONES

BONECHI

GLOSSARY

BENCHES
Architectural elements that are part of the structures flanking the central patio of the game ground in the pelota court, with a ground plan in the form of a capital I.

CE ACATL TOPILTZIN
Governor of Tula, son of Mixcóatl, chief of the Toltecs, and of Chimalma; he was the high priest of the god Quetzalcóatl and preserved his calendar name "Ce Acatl" (One reed), the sign of the year he was born in, and Topiltzin which means "our prince".

CENOTE
Deposit of water springing from a subeterranean torrent which comes to the surface in the form of a well or depression, typical of the calcareous soil of the Yucatán peninsula.

CHAC
The Maya god of rain.

CHAC-MOOL
Half-reclining statue with thick-set legs and head, thought by some to represent the divine messenger between man and the gods.

CHALCHIUTLICUE
"She of the jade skirt", goddess of water, rivers and lakes; she was the feminine counterpart of Tlaloc.

CHENES
Maya style of architecture.

CHULTÚN
Means cistern, in Maya language.

COATEPANTLI
Wall of serpents, from the Náhuatl *cóatl*; serpent and *tepantli*: wall, it is the name given to the serpents represented around various pre-Columbian temples in the different cultures in the Valley of Mexico.

COATLICUE
"She of the serpent skirt"; among the Aztecs or Mexicas she was the mother goddess of different divinities, such as Huitzilopochtli, tutelary god of the Mexicas, conceived miraculously.

CODZ-POOP
The most important building in Kabáh, Yucatán, whose name means "rolled mat", due perhaps to the form of its staircase which looks like a roll, or the curved nose of Chac, the god of rain.

DIOS VIEJO
God of fire, also known as Huehuetéotl in the Nàhuatl tongue, who was worshipped by different pre-Columbian cultures.

FACADE, AIRBORN
Also known as flying facade. The extremely high cresting found on various buildings in Palenque.

FEATHERED SERPENT
Also called Plumed Serpent. Meaning of the name of the god Quetzalcóatl.

HUITZILOPOCHTLI
"The humming bird of the left", god of the sun, the deity of war and tutelar divinity of the Aztecs.

ITZÁES
Ancient Mayas who arrived in the Yucatán peninsula from Petén in Guatemala and subsequently settled in Chichén Itzá.

IX CHEL
Mayan goddess of the moon and childbirth.

KUKULKÁN
Mayan name of Quetzalcóatl, the feathered serpent.

NÁHUATL
Language spoken by the Nahua group.

NEW FIRE
Ceremony held by the Mexicas or Aztecs, each 52 years, duration of a cycle on their calendar; in which all fires were extinguished, and the priests lighted the new fire on the Hill of the Star (Cerro de la Estrella), in Iztapalapa, and at dawn the red-hot coals were taken to the hearths of all the houses.

ONE REED
Name of one of the years of the Nahua calendar, which returned after a determined period of time.

PALMAS
Stone sculpture, of the cultures of the Gulf Coast of Mexico, so-called for the spreading form of the upper part that calls to mind a palm frond.

PUTUNES
Integrants of an ancient Maya group, the Putún.

PUUC
Word that means mountain ridge, also the name given to one of the Mayan architectural styles.

QUETZAL
Bird with showy plumage which lives in the forests of southern Mexico and Central America.

QUETZALCÓATL
Originally a Toltec divinity and subsequently his worship extended to different sites in Meso America.

QUETZALPAPALOTL
Name of the butterfly-birds which decorate the palace of Quetzalpapalotl in Teotihuacán.

RÍO BEC
Mayan architectural style.

"SMALL SMILING HEADS"
Sculpture characteristic of the culture of El Tajín, in the zone of Gulf of Mexico, characterized by the fact that they are shown smiling or laughing, an unusual example of pre-Columbian sculpture.

TABLERO-ESCAPULARIO
A projecting plane used in the decoration of some parts of a building. Rectangular in form it consists of two planes, where sunken spaces alternate with vertical or inclined cornices, with a decorative motif of an open W.

TALUD-TABLERO
Sloping wall surface combined with a projecting plane used to decorate various parts of buildings.

TENOCHTITLÁN
Capital of the Aztecs who settled in the Valley of Mexico.

TEZCATLIPOCA
"The smoking mirror", one of the principal divinities of the Náhuatl-speaking group.

TLÁLOC
God of rain and water; one of the most widely worshipped in Meso-America.

TLALOCAN
The paradise of Tláloc, destined for those who died drowned, as a result of misfortune or tempests.

TZOMPANTLI
Structure used to place the skulls of the sacrificed victims.

XIUES
Plural of Xiu, the reigning family in Uxmal, Yucatán, during the Maya-Toltec period and that of Mexican Absorption.

XOCHIPILLO
"The prince of flowers", divinity associated with flowers, games and dance.

INTRODUCTION

When the New World was discovered at the end of the 15th century, the Europeans were astonished by the civilizations they encountered, little imagining that they were the result of an evolution that had begun several thousand years before the birth of Christ.

Part of the territory of what at present is the Republic of Mexico was occupied by civilizations which developed along similar lines and which shared many of their basic characteristics. This entire area now goes by the name of Meso-America.

The development of the Meso-American cultures has been divided into three stages by archaeologists: preclassic: 2000 B.C.-1000 B.C.; classic: 100 B.C.-A.D. 900 and postclassic: A.D. 900-1519.

The preclassic stage began with agriculture, as far back as the year 2000 B.C., when the first villages were established and large groups which lived together and required a more complex social organization were formed. However, not until the year 1000 B.C. did the Olmecs of the coast of the Gulf of Mexico create the first civilization in which many of the traits which distinguish the Meso-American cultures could be identified: it was among the Olmecs that large stone sculpture, writing, organized ceremonial centers, and the cult of a jaguar god were to be found.

The classic period began in the early years of the Christian era: this was when the Meso-American cultures acquired distinct regional characteristics, and manifested their own styles in architecture, painting, and sculpture in stone and clay. Cities such as Teotihuacán, Palenque and Monte Albán, to name only a few, were built at this time.

The postclassic period began when the large classic centers were abandoned and some of them destroyed. When the groups that had lived there emigrated to other regions, they took with them many of the characteristics they had developed in the large metropolises: some of these groups arrived as far as Central America, such as the Pipiles and the Nicaraos, Náhuatl speaking tribes, to be found in El Salvador and Nicaragua in the 16th century.

The books (codexes) written during this period, documents which record historical, astronomical and religious events, have survived up to our time. But for an understanding of the postclassic period the importance of the Chichimecs in Meso-America cannot be overlooked.

Groups of hunters who lived in the north erupted violently and left their mark on the civilized life of Meso-America, provoking changes in all aspects, changes which make it possible to explain the development of the Mexica or Aztec people.

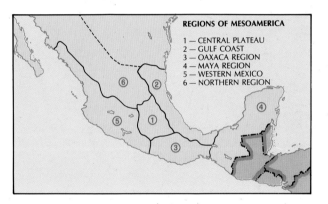

REGIONS OF MESOAMERICA

1 — CENTRAL PLATEAU
2 — GULF COAST
3 — OAXACA REGION
4 — MAYA REGION
5 — WESTERN MEXICO
6 — NORTHERN REGION

CHRONOLOGY OF THE CULTURES IN PRECOLUMBIAN MEXICO

PERIODS	CULTURES
PRECLASSIC: 2000 B.C. to 100 A.D.	WEST (1500 B.C.) LOWER TLATILCO (1250-1000 B.C.) OLMEC (1200-500 B.C.) MIDDLE TLATILCO (1000-800 B.C.) WEST (600 B.C.) UPPER TLATILCO (800-100 B.C.) ZAPOTEC (800 B.C.-100 A.D.)
CLASSIC: 100 to 900 A.D.	TEOTIHUACAN (700-100 A.D.) WEST (200-650 or 900 A.D.) ZAPOTEC (200-800 A.D.) EL TAJIN (300-900 A.D.) NORTHERN MEXICO (400-1000 A.D.)
POSTCLASSIC: 900 to 1519 A.D.	TOLTEC (900-1300 A.D.) MIXTEC (800-1519 A.D.) WEST: TARASCOS (900-1519 A.D.) HUAXTEC (900-1519 A.D.) NORTHERN MEXICO (1110-1300 A.D.) MEXICA or AZTEC (1110-1519 A.D.)

CHRONOLOGY OF THE MAYA CULTURE

PRECLASSIC	OR FORMATIVE (500 B.C.-325 A.D.)
CLASSIC	EARLY CLASSIC (325-625 A.D.) FLOURISHING (625-800 A.D.) COLLAPSE OR DECADENCE (800-925 A.D.)
POSTCLASSIC	INTERREGNUM or TRANSITIONAL (925-975 A.D.) MEXICAN or MAYA-TOLTEC (975-1200 A.D.) OF MEXICAN ABSORPTION (1200-1540 A.D.)

MUSEO NACIONAL DE ANTROPOLOGIA DE LA CIUDAD DE MEXICO

In the 1964 the old museum which had existed in the center of the city since 1864 was transferred to the Bosque de Chapultepec. The present museum derives from one of the first in the American continent, founded in Mexico in 1825.

The rooms on the top floor of the modern building are dedicated to contemporary tribal groups. The lower floor, in eleven rooms, narrates the story of Archaeology in Mexico, and also provides an introduction to Anthropology.

Various doors lead from these rooms to the large central patio. The Introductory Hall and the Meso-American Room provide a panorama — the former, of the distinct branches that go into the making of the science of Anthropology, and the latter, of the cultural evolution of civilization in pre-Columbian Mexico. The five rooms that follow show, in chronological order, the evolution of the human groups which occupied the center of the country from Prehistory up to the arrival of the Spaniards in 1519.

Female figurine in clay (1100-600 B.C.); woman was associated with fertility, which is why she was so frequently represented in this period.

Stone mask with a mosaic of turquoise, shell and obsidian; a technique first used by the Teotihuacans.

Censer or, perhaps, a domestic altar with representations of two mythological Teotihuacán animals.

Funerary mask in clay, from Teotihuacán; the butterfly-shaped nose pendent is related to fire.

Toltec sculpture in clay; a human head emerging from the jaws of a coyote.

Reproduction of the stone bench from the Quemado Palace of Tula.

Room of the Origins

Shown here are the first signs of the presence of man in part of the national territory, as well as bones of extinct animals that lived with the inhabitants of the time.

Preclassic Room

In the year 2000 B.C. the first villages were established and corn, squash and beans began to be cultivated. Archaeological excavations have brought to light principally objects in clay: female figurines related to fertility cults, pottery, and tools in stone and bone. All these were found as offerings to the dead, buried underneath the floor of the huts.

Significant changes took place between the years 1000 and 100 B.C., when commerce with far-off regions began, resulting in the diffusion of new elements and enriching the local cultures. Religious concepts became more complex, expressed in ceremonial architecture, the representations of the first gods, rites such as the game of pelota, and progress in astronomical knowledge, which led to a calendar whose scope was agricultural and ritual, and the invention of writing to record it.

Teotihuacán Room

The classic period (100 B.C.-A.D. 900) witnessed an extraordinary leap ahead with respect to the precedent period. The great religious centers and the cities arose, covering wide areas with orderly constructions furnished with patios and plazas, oriented along predetermined axes based on the cardinal points, evidence of a long tradition in the study of the stars.

The finest example of this period is Teotihuacán, the « City of the Gods », so called for its legends and size — as shown by the fact that it extended over all of 40 square km. In its architecture the perfection of the building technique is accompanied by an original style in which sloping elements are combined with vertical elements (talud-tablero) to form the stepped foundations on which the temples were set.

A city like Teotihuacán is the result of a society that is highy evolved in its social, as well as political, and religious organization, with an economy that was sound enough to support priests, builders, painters, sculptors, potters, etc.

The governing class at its head probably consisted of priest-kings who monopolized the use of the large constructions and art in general and controlled the manufacture and commercialization of the products as well as knowledge of the stars, writing, the use of the calendar and the rites and ceremonies dedicated to the gods.

Toltec Room

At the end of the classic period many cities were destroyed as a result of internal conflicts, and the inhabitants moved to more distant regions, while other migrating groups, coming from the north, invaded the area, fusing with the more cultured inhabitants; new cities with different characteristics thus sprang up and the early postclassic period began (A.D. 900-1250).

Coatlicue, « The Lady of the Serpent Skirt », Aztec goddess of the Earth.

The Sun Stone or Aztec Calendar Stone commemorates the fifth era of Aztec mythology.

Another of the forms used by the Aztecs to represent the goddess Coatlicue; her emaciated countenance is a sign of her relationship with the netherworld.

Xochipilli, Aztec god of flowers, music and dance. He unites elements of life and death.

The ritual pottery offered by the Aztecs to their gods was finely modeled and painted.

One of these were the Toltec-Chichimecs, who founded their capital in Tula, city of Ce Acatl Topiltzin Quetzalcóatl: « One Reed, Our Prince, Quetzalcóatl », the name given to the governor, who was both the priest of this deity and the hero of many myths which survived among the Aztecs until the arrival of the Spaniards and were written down by the monks who came with them.

These new times brought change in all aspects of life. Political organization was dominated by the warrior class which was of utmost importance and undertook territorial conquests aimed at imposing religious beliefs and an economic domination. Gods and men were depicted as warriors; the number of human sacrifices increased and hearts were included in the decoration in the bas-reliefs on the buildings.

Mexica or Aztec Room

After lengthy migrations from the north of Meso-America, the Aztecs or Mexicas, of Chichimec origin, arrived at a small island in the center of the lake which covered what is now called the Valley of Mexico. There they founded their city which they called México-Tenochtitlán.

This site allowed them to coexist with a number of political and cultural centers which had already existed for some time on the shores of the lake, and to participate as mercenaries in the wars they were engaged in against each other. It was doubtless their valor and warlike spirit which made it possible for the Aztecs to acquire the predominant position they occupied in the 15th and 16th centuries.

They ruled over a great number of towns which, subjected to the Aztecs empire, were required to pay tribute in agricultural products, animals, gold and silver, cotton cloth, jade beads, uniforms and weapons for the warriors, and manpower for construction and the armies. It was all carefully organized through the use of books and registers and inspectors sent to the most distant places.

The streets of the Aztecs capital, built on the lake, were canals and transportation was via canoe, which inspired some of the conquistadores to compare it to Venice. The principal religious and ceremonial buildings were situated in a sacred enclosure, surrounded by a wall decorated with carved serpents, and containing pyramids such as the Great Temple, dedicated to the two gods: Tláloc, god of rain, and Huitzilopochtli, god of war; and other temples consecrated to various gods, as well as civic-administrative buildings; the school for priests, the Palace of the Governor, the Pelota Court and the zoological gardens and many others.

Above: jade mask of the Zapotec god Murciélago.

Below: Zapotec sculpture in clay, found in Tomb 113 in Monte Albán.

Detail of a clay urn, representing the Zapotec Dios Viejo.

Reproduction of Tomb 104 in Monte Albán; the niches are characteristic features of all the Zapotec tombs. The wall paintings depict gods and animals.

The Aztec or Mexica nation was the heir to a 3000-year-old cultural tradition, which can be identified in some of its religious concepts, political and economic institutions which preserve influences from cultures such as the Toltec, Teotihuacán and even Olmec.

Notwithstanding, the art forms reveal an extraordinary originality and display a style in which great power and a great individuality are fused. The last Aztecs governor and the city of Tenochtitlán fell into the hands of the Spanish conquistadores on August 13, 1521.

Oaxaca Room

In the pre-Columbian period the region now called Oaxaca was a place of great cultural diversity whose people maintained distinct traditions and languages, with Zapotec and Mixtec prevailing.

The history of this region is generally based on what is known of places such as Monte Albán. This is why the dates of its development are used for the entire area. Monte Albán I (1000-300 B.C.), contemporary with the village cultures of the preclassic period, presents Olmec influence.

Monte Albán II (330 B.C.-A.D. 1) reveals progress in writing and in the calendar, recorded in the stone steles.

Monte Albán III (A.D. 300-900), the period of its classic apogee, is that of the greatest development in the Zapotec centers of the valleys of Oaxaca, where large buildings and sculpture in a distinctive style were produced, excelling in funerary ar-

Mixtec pectoral in gold with turquoise mosaic.

Shield covered with thin gold lamina, found in a tomb in Zaachila. Oaxaca.

chitecture. A' great number of tombs were built below buildings and patios and it is to these that most of the art creation was dedicated: the decoration with wall paintings and the pottery « urns » with gods and priests meant to protect the dead.

But the protection of these gods was not always sufficient, for the tombs were opened and plundered by the Mixtecs.

They developed independently up to the time when they decided to invade the Zapotec territory, occupying sites which without doubt enjoyed an ancestral prestige, and where they deposited their dead. In these reused tombs, the Mixtecs placed rich offerings: objects in gold, silver, turquoise and coral, and delicate fragments of finely worked bone.

The Mixtecs created a sequence of ritual and genealogical books, of which some, happily, have survived to the 20th century, giving us an idea, in their colored images, of the feelings their gods and governors ispired.

Room of the Gulf Cultures

The first civilization of ancient Mexico and one of the first on the American continent developed in the southern part of the coast of the Gulf of Mexico.

During the years 1200-600 B.C. the Olmecs began many of the religious traditions and some of the most important skills that were to be accepted and developed later on by other cultures.

Complex religious concepts are expressed in some of the finest stone sculpture to be found in Meso-American art: the principle of writing and the calendar; large organized centers and mythological figures such as the jaguar associated with the earth and the netherworld, the serpent, related to water and fertility.

During the classic period, various cultures with distinctive features of their own existed in the central region of the Gulf Coast. A great artistic wealth found expression in architectural creations such as El Tajín, or in fine

large-scale clay sculpture, as well as in some of lesser size but with traits that had never before appeared, such as the « small smiling heads ». The ceremonial rites associated with the game of pelota acquired a fundamental importance; a series of stone sculpture, yokes-axes-palmas, and the construction of buildings with fine bas-reliefs are related to this game.

The Totonacs dominated the history of the Gulf Coast from the year 1000 on. Their capital, Cempoala, was the first city Cortez and his soldiers entered in 1519.

The Huastecos, who occupied· the north coast and part of the territory towards the west, were heirs to the coastal tradition which symbolized a place of flowering and fertility.

The Huastec area was divided into various small independent dominions which now and then united to combat the common enemy: the Aztec empire.

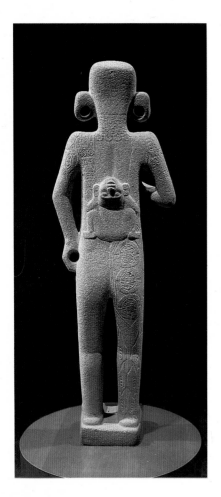
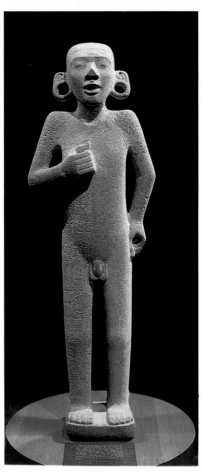

Above: offering representing a scene of an Olmec ceremony from La Venta.

Below: the « Adolescent » from Tamuín, San Luis Potosí, representing the god Quetzalcóatl in his appellation of the planet Venus.

Some of the finest sculptured Maya lintels are to be found in Yaxchilán, Chiapas. On Lintel 26 (726 A.D.) an important personage seems to be receiving the offering of a jaguar mask.

Maya Room

The Maya culture occupied the most extensive geographical area in Meso-America, overflowed the Mexican territory into part of Central America; as a result there were marked regional differences which were manifested, in particular, in distinct artistic styles.

The Mayas produced imposing structures, thanks to the fact that they used materials such as limestone. The stone made it possible to obtain a type of roof which endowed the buildings with a unique style and in addition facilitated the preservation throughout the centuries.

The period in which the great Maya ceremonial centers and cities reached their zenith was between the years 300-1000; architectural complexes, generally set up on large platforms, spread out over extensive areas. Some of the temples were so tall that they seemed to compete with the trees of the tropical forests that frequently surrounded them. At the same time other low horizontal structures contained dozens of apartments in which the priests and governors of these places lived. All were decorated with figures in stone or stucco that covered the walls and ceiling, and in some cases with wall paintings depicting religious or historical scenes, unmatched for their beauty in America. The steles were part of the architectural com-

The Olmecs were the first great sculptors in stone in pre-Columbian Mexico; the statue of the « Wrestler ».

plexes, and their use was not limited to the Maya, even though they achieved a distinctive expression here, which served to record important historical, political or religious events.

The steles have provided us with a knowledge of the writing and the use of the calendar. Maya writing, based on hieroglyphics, combined phonetic and ideographic principles.

The Mayas had various calendars: the ritual calendar, of 260 days, and the solar calendar, of 360 days and a fraction. But thanks to their knowledge of astronomy and mathematics, they also discovered the Venusian cycle of 584 days and established a register which counted the passage of time starting from an arbitrarily established date, like the year zero for western culture.

Dates were annotated in a vigesimal system with numbers of distinct values. Bar-five; dot-one; shell-zero; placed in vertical columns, with a specific value according to the position occupied.

Great changes took place in the Maya culture after the year 900. The Yucatán peninsula became enormously important and a sequence of extraordinary centers and cities were concentrated there. Internal changes were added to those that were taking place throughout Meso-America: groups from the Central Plateau brought to the south the cult of Quetzalcóatl, whom the Mayas called Kukulkán. Various architectural-sculptural styles arose at this point, such as the « Chenes », the « Puuc » and the « Río Bec », and commerce expanded, especially via sea, reaching as far as Central America.

Left: hollow Maya sculpture in clay with a mask of the sun god, found in Palenque.

Center: figurine from the island of Jaina, Campeche.

Right: polychrome clay urn, depicting the Maya god of rain.

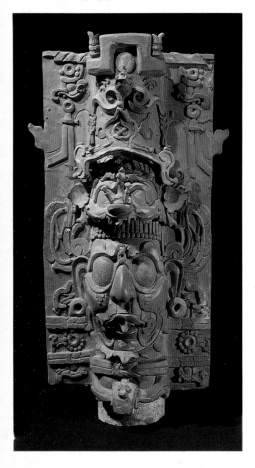  

Room of the North

In the pre-Columbian period various groups that were culturally less developed than their neighbors to the south existed in the north of the country. Some of them present Meso-American influences in a more highly developed architecture, as is the case of the Quemada and the Calchihuites, in what is now the state of Zacatecas.

In other places, such as Casas Grandes (Paquime), Chihuahua, a culture developed that revealed influences from the southeast of the United States, since both present similar buildings constructed in adobe.

The men and women of the governing class, as well as the funerary offerings, were the principal theme of the Maya sculptors of the island of Jaina.

Below, left: stone disc found in Chinkultic, Chiapas. At the center is a pelota player surrounded by glyphs and numbers. The game of pelota, an important ceremony, was present in almost all the cultures of pre-Columbian Mexico.

Below, right: stone sculpture of the god Kukulkán emerging from the maw of a serpent, a frequent theme in the Maya-Toltec period.

Mosaic in turquoise, mother of pearl and jadeite, found in the substructure of the Castillo of Chichén Itzá.

Stone sculpture of the god Kukulkán called the Queen of Uxmal.

Bonampak, in Chiapas, is considered the Sistine Chapel of pre-Columbian painting. Scene of a battle between Maya warriors. Reproduction in the Museo Nacional de Antropología.

West Room

The western region of Mexico developed independently from the rest of Meso-America with architecturally modest ceremonial centers, but with a rich development in clay sculpture.

A profound preoccupation with the dead is revealed, reflected in the construction of tombs excavated deep underground.

In 1250 Michoacán began to be preponderant in the historical scene of the west insomuch as the Tarascos succeeded in competing with the powerful Mexicas and resisted their expansion, keeping them within just limits.

The settlers of Casas Grandes, Chihuahua, in the north of the country, produced simple vases, decorated with geometric motifs.

The inhabitants of the West of Mexico were magnificent sculptors of animals which they made as funerary offerings.

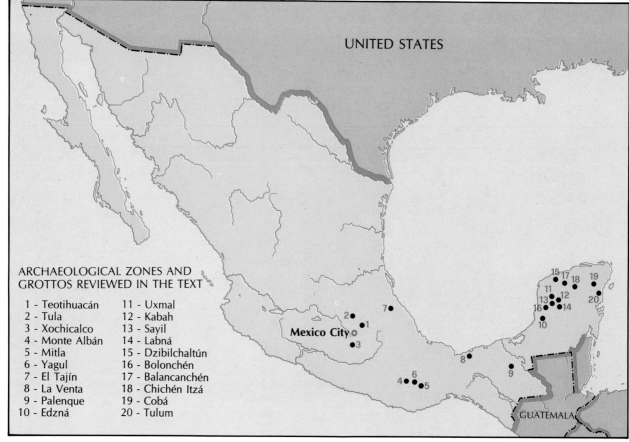

ARCHAEOLOGICAL ZONES AND
GROTTOS REVIEWED IN THE TEXT

1 - Teotihuacán
2 - Tula
3 - Xochicalco
4 - Monte Albán
5 - Mitla
6 - Yagul
7 - El Tajín
8 - La Venta
9 - Palenque
10 - Edzná

11 - Uxmal
12 - Kabah
13 - Sayil
14 - Labná
15 - Dzibilchaltún
16 - Bolonchén
17 - Balancanchén
18 - Chichén Itzá
19 - Cobá
20 - Tulum

UNITED STATES

Mexico City

GUATEMALA

Teotihuacán in the 19th century as seen by José María Velasco, one of the best Mexican landscape painters.

The Avenue of the Dead, main axis of Teotihuacán, is two km. long. On the north it terminates in the Pyramid of the Moon.

TEOTIHUACAN

In a semiarid valley of the Central Plateau, surrounded by hills, 2000 m. above the sea, the greatest city of all pre-Columbian cultures, Teotihuacán, was built. It was here according to legend that all arts originated, wisdom, skills and the gods and their beliefs.

But Teotihuacán did not just suddenly appear out of nothing. Its extensive development was begun in 200 B.C. by the founders who built an initial small pyramid now under that of the Sun, and who may have dedicated themselves to the working of obsidian.

AVENUE OF THE DEAD

It is the axis of the city and measures 2.5 kilometers from north to south. The slope of the ground, higher in the north, is compensated for by large terraces and flights of stairs. On either side, along this avenue 40 m. wide, staircases leading to the different building complexes were built. The north part of the avenue terminates in the Complex of the Plaza of the Moon, while the Ciudadela is at the south end.

In its second phase Teotihuacán covered an extension of almost 20 sq. km. and it has been calculated that it must have had between 25 and 30,000 inhabitants and twenty-three inhabited architectural complexes.

GREAT PLAZA OF THE CIUDADELA

South of the Avenue of the Dead, exactly aligned with the Pyramid of the Sun, is a large sunken plaza, 400 m. per side, which was the architectural high point of the city, both thanks to the way in which architecture and sculpture were combined on its main building, and in its social function, for it could contain thousands of people for the religious ceremonies.

Recent excavation (1980-1982) has revealed previously unknown aspects of the Ciudadela such as structures which served as dwellings for the priests and governors, as well as the remains of sacrificed victims, their hands tied, on either side of the Pyramid of Quetzalcóatl, which modified current ideas regarding the religion of Teotihuacán.

The oldest structure of the Ciudadela is the Pyramid of Quetzalcóatl, later covered by another.

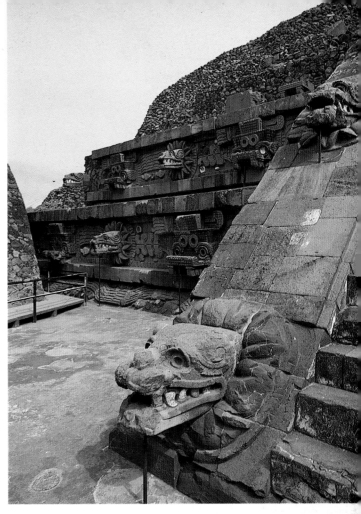

PYRAMID OF QUETZALCOATL

The six tiers of the building were constructed in *talud* and *tablero* but, in this case, both *tableros* and *taludes* are completely covered by sculpture and bas-reliefs, unique for Teotihuacán since normally they were covered with painting. The short *taludes* have a feathered serpent and, on either side of the body, shells and snails relating to fertility.

Projecting from the wall, on the *tableros*, heads of the gods Quetzalcóatl and Tláloc, his eyes decorated with fragments of obsidian, alternate; on the flat part of the *tablero*, the same serpent as on the *talud*, now identified by the rattles on its tail, is also accompanied by shells and snails.

Above, left: part of the Plaza of the Ciudadela, one of the largest urban and religious complexes in Teotihuacán.

Below, left: the Pyramid of Quetzalcóatl, decorated with heads of Tláloc and Quetzalcóatl.

Above, right: the tiers or sections in talud-tablero, decorated with shells, snails and feathered serpents.

Below, right: head of Quetzalcóatl, « feathered serpent », adorned with petals or plumes.

PYRAMID OF THE SUN

This enormous pyramid, which measures 222 by 225 meters at its base and is 63 meters high, is one of the tallest of pre-Columbian times.

This pyramid furnished the entire city with its orientation, calculated according to the position of the sun, and in a determined period of the year the light of the sun falls vertically over the center of the structure.

TEPANTITLA

On its walls this palace bears a representation of the paradise of the god of Rain, the Tlalocan where everything is fertile and flourishing; large figures of priests with ornaments of the god Tláloc cover the walls, in line with a symmetry that was obligatory in Teotihuacán. In the lower part of the mural, the Teotihuacanos are shown in various activities, playing, full of heavenly bliss as befits such a place.

Above left: the Pyramid of the Sun consists of approx. a millon cubic m. of earth, and its construction must have required 10,000 laborers for a period of ten years.

Below left: the Teotihuacán concept of paradise, painted of the wall of the Palace of Tepantitla.

The Avenue of the Dead.

On Platform 16 of the Avenue of the Dead, a feline, perhaps a delfied puma, is connected with certain forces of nature.

The Pyramid of the Moon; like all the other structures in Teotihuacán, it is composed of various superposed constructions dating to different periods. In the foreground, the altar in the center of its plaza.

Above, right: the older sections (sloping) and the later sections (talud-tablero) of the Pyramid of the Moon can here be discerned.

Below, right: many visitors climb to the top of the Pyramid of the Moon for a panorama of the Valley of Teotihuacán.

PYRAMID OF THE MOON

Built on a platform 120 by 150 m. at the base and 43 m. high, it stands on the highest part of the terrain so as to be on a level with the Pyramid of the Sun. There are two stages in its construction, which can easily be noted. The first presents inclined levels of differing heights with a flight of steps on the front; later, other structures were added, in which the levels were built by combining two elements: one inclined and the other vertical, called *talud-tablero*. It should be noted that technical progress in construction methods was necessary to achieve these buildings, for ex. tree trunks were used to form internal containing walls for the filler material.

The large sculpture of Chalchiutlicue, water goddess, now in the Museo Nacional de Antropología in Mexico City was found in the Plaza of the Moon.

The city reached its apogee in the third and fourth periods (A.D. 150-450).

The splendor achieved by Teotihuacán at this time was marvelous and its influence, in architecture and in art, reached as far as Guatemala in Central America. Other Meso-American cultures imitated its *talud-tablero* construction as well as its style of pottery and rendered worship to its gods: Tláloc, god of rain, and the Feathered Serpent, related to fertility. Traders and pilgrims arrived in this city, combining business with religion in concurrence with the great ceremonies that must have been celebrated here.

In this stage Teotihuacán grew to 42 sq. km. and its population increased to 200,000. The entire Avenue of the Dead was covered with buildings and the palaces where the priests and governors lived were to be found in the ceremonial zone and in the environs.

Left: the bird carved on the pillars of the patio received the name of Quetzalpapalotl; the eyes are encrusted with obsidian.

Right: red and green color covers the stone, infusing life in the animal represented.

Above, left: entrance to the Palace of Quetzalpapalotl, flanked by serpent heads.

Below, left: the inner patio of the Palace, one of the loveliest buildings in Teotihuacán.

PALACE OF QUETZALPAPALOTL

Destroyed and burned by the Teotihuacans themselves, this palace was reconstructed in the excavations of 1962-1964. It forms part of the Plaza of the Moon and was undoubtedly inhabited by priests. There is an antechamber with paintings which leads to a patio decorated with pilasters and a bird in the bas-reliefs that seems to be a quetzal. The roof is formed of a *tablero* supported by pillars, and above the former are the merlons, a frequent element in Teotihuacán.

There are other palaces, not reconstructed, in the area that gravitates around the ceremonial center: Tepantitla, Atetelco, Tetitla, Tlamimilolpa and Zacuala, among others. Decorated with paintings on all the walls, each one presents a different pictorial style and a distinctive theme, although always concerning religious and ritual aspects.

Rear patio of the Palace of Quetzalpapalotl, called Patio of the Tigers. The priests lived in similar buildings.

Above, right: a jaguar with a feather headdress blowing a marine snail. Painting in the Palace of the Jaguars.

Below, right: different styles and colors characterize Teotihuacán wall painting.

The Atlantes, representations of divinities, hold weapons in both hands and have butterfly pectorals; the heads terminate in bands of stars and plumes, signs of their celestial character.

Above, left: the Temple of the Morning Star, in Tula, Hidalgo; the columns in the foreground supported the roof of the vestibule.

Below, left: the Coatepantli, « wall of serpents », with its stuccoed and painted reliefs, framed by fretwork and snail-shaped merlons.

TULA

The city of Quetzalcóatl was built on an area of the Central Plateau full of external influences, both from the Chichimeca people, seminomadic hunters and extemporary farmers, as well as contacts which arrived from the Gulf Coast of Mexico, proceeding from the southern regions, such as the Maya.

The name Toltec meant « enlightened being » and « artist ». The god of the civilized world was Quetzalcóatl, « feathered serpent », a concept which implies the fusion of two elements such as earth-sky, darkness-light, morning star-evening star, a union represented in Tula in a great variety of forms.

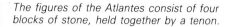
The figures of the Atlantes consist of four blocks of stone, held together by a tenon.

Above, right: the architectural style of Xochicalco, composed of a tall sloping wall and a small cornice.

Below, right: the Pyramid of the Feathered Serpents, in Xochicalco, masterpiece of the fusion of architecture and scuplture.

THE TEMPLE OF TLAHUIZCALPANTECUTLI

Oriented north-south, it is preceded by a vestibule of almost a hundred pillars which relate it to the Temple of the Warriors in Chichén Itzá, in Yucatán. The sloping ramparts were faced with thin stone panels carved with rows of jaguars and coyotes as well as eagles and vultures.
The bas-reliefs with birds alternate with others representing the god Quetzalcóatl as man-bird-serpent.
The temple, destroyed in pre-Columbian times by the Chichimec invaders of Tula, had eight stone supports; four columns which represented Venus as the Morning Star, called Atlantes, and each formed of four sections fitted into each other for a total height of 4.6 meters.
The Coatepantli, or « wall of serpents », encloses the anterior temple on the north. A row of serpents, an allegory of the earth, is executed in stucco.

XOCHICALCO

« The place of the House of Flowers » was mentioned in the 16th century by the Spaniards as a ceremonial center of great antiquity and importance. The buildings are particularly striking, especially that of the « Feathered Serpent » dating to the late classic period, which some scholars consider the loveliest in pre-Columbian Mexico.
The Pyramid of the Feathered Serpent, consisting of a sloping rampart, terminating in a projecting cornice, has reliefs of large undulating serpents on its four sides, together with richly adorned figures accompanied by calendar dates in which Mayan, Zapotec, Mixtec and Nahua elements are combined. It would thus appear to have been a meeting place for astronomer sages who came from far-off regions for various important ceremonies, probably including that of the New Fire which initiated a new life cycle of 52 years.

MONTE ALBAN

Since 1800 B.C. the region of Oaxaca had been rich in cultural traditions, an obligatory passage for the traders who were on their way from the Gulf Coast to the Valley of Mexico or the Maya regions. This led to a continuous exchange of cultural elements, which mingled with the local development and created the rich and complex Zapotec culture.

Monte Albán was the most important center in the entire region. Situated on a group of hills 2000 meters above sea level, it dominated the rich valleys which surrounded it and supported it economically. The strategic site facilitated defense and celebrations of religious type. The Zapotecs leveled off the summit and cut away the rocky sides to create an extraordinary rectangular plaza 300 m. wide and 200 m. deep, surrounded by platforms with broad stairways, pyramids, temples and, at one end, the pelota court.

Initially a civic-religious center, it gradually grew throughout its long life, which began more or less 800 B.C., until it was a city of 6.5 sq. km. with patios, palaces and tombs for the ruling classes, as well as small platforms for the simpler houses which were built on the slopes of the hills.

TOMBS OF THE GOVERNORS

Hundreds of tombs of different periods are to be found everywhere in Monte Albán: underneath the patios and temple and palace stairways, rectangular or cruciform in shape, but always adorned with niches for offerings in the side walls.

Some of them are completely frescoed: no. 104 and 105, with priests and gods together with sacred animals and calendar dates, are painted in many colors in which red with its solar symbolism predominates.

The entrance is protected by plaques and urns, placed in the upper part, with gods or personages associated with the dead. Tomb no. 7, sealed after it had been built, was

The Gran Plaza in Monte Albán is the result of various periods of construction. In the foreground, the North Platform with its sunken patio.

occupied during the 14th century by the Mixtecs, who deposited in it an important chief accompanied by one of the richest offerings to be found on the American continent: jewellery in gold, turquoise, jade and shell, together with other objects in alabaster, pottery and bone.

Left: entrance to Tomb 104 in Monte Albán; the urn, which represents a priest wearing the headdress of the god Murciélago, protected the remains deposited here.

Below: painting in Tomb 105: a procession of priests dressed in Teotihuacán style, bearing ornaments that symbolize the god Tláloc.

Right: the paintings in Tomb 104 with large figures of priests, with headdresses of serpents and plumes.

*The extreme north end of the Gran Plaza in
Monte Albán.*

*Numerous steles were sculptured in the different
periods of Monte Albán; they record historical events.*

*Above, left: the Pelota Court in Monte Albán, one of
the oldest in Meso-America. Its sloping walls were
covered with stucco and painted red.*

*Below, left: the Zapotec architectural style created the
oldest staircases in pre-Columbian Mexico.*

THE PELOTA COURT OF MONTE ALBAN

This is one of the constructions dedicated to this ritual
game, the oldest in pre-Columbian Mexico. Various feature differ from some of the others, such as the niches in
the opposite corners.

Above, left: the Building of the Danzantes, one of the first built in Monte Albán.

Below, left: the Danzantes, reliefs that show Olmec influence both in their style as well as in the physical type they represent.

Some of the reliefs of the Danzantes have glyphs in Zapotec writing that have not yet been deciphered.

In group IV of Monte Albán, the « tablero-escapulario » terminates the staircases.

LOS DANZANTES

Heavy stone slabs were used to face one of the first structures built in Monte Albán (400 B.D.). They are carved with bas-reliefs of nude men, with contorted extremities, who seem to be dancing, but they might also be captives accompanied by hieroglyphic inscriptions.

Above: in period III-B (350-700 A.D.) the construction of the Great Plaza in Monte Albán was finished.

Below: Mound G, at the center of the plaza.

Above, right: Mound J whose unique form stands out among all the buildings in the plaza. A series of figured stones on its inner walls record military conquests.

Below, right: the dimensions of the staircases built by the Zapotecs can here be properly appreciated.

MUSEO REGIONAL OF OAXACA

The Convent of Santo Domingo whose construction, begun in 1570, was terminated in the second half of the 17th century.

Cloister of the Convent; site of the Museo Regional of Oaxaca.

Among the jewels found in Tomb 7 in Monte Albán, were various necklaces in gold, coral and pearls.

Gold pectoral, one of the most important pieces in the museum since the value of its complicated decoration is enhanced by that of its calendar significance.

Below, left: gold pendants made in the lost wax process, which allowed the artist to achieve great refinement in execution.

Below, center: the animals represented in this gold pendant always include a religious symbol.

Below, right: the different parts of this gold pendant are related to the meaning of the pre-Columbian pelota game.

  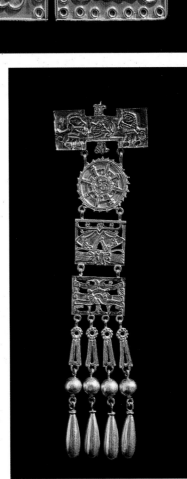

Above: North Complex, or the Iglesia, in Mitla.

Left: detail of the fretwork mosaics.

Above, right: facade of the Hall of the Columns.

Below, right: inner patio of the Palace of the Columns.

MITLA

The site of the residence of the Zapotec high priest during the 16th century lies 40 km. from Oaxaca, and was described by the first Spaniards who arrived in this region. The priest, incarnation of the god, lived apart, studying the stars to interpret their designs and regulate agricultural labors, as well as the ceremonies which had to accompany them; he was held in awe by all, including the governor.

There are five groups of buildings in Mitla, mostly dwellings set around internal patios.

The most important and best preserved structure is the Palace of the Columns, so-called because it consists of a broad narrow hall of monolithic columns and an internal courtyard.

Above: North Building of the Group of the Columns in Mitla.

Left: mask from Oaxaca used in traditional fiestas.

Above, right: the Pelota Court in Yagul.

Below, right: the Palace of the Six Patios, in Yagul.

YAGUL

Called « Pueblo Viejo » in some of the Oaxaca chronicles of the 19th century, Yagul can be seen from a great distance, raised on a terraced hill. At the top, the acropolis, surrounded by the remains of a wall both natural and man made; lower down the palaces and temples, together with dwellings with thick walls that were stuccoed and painted, where the elite lodged, and in the lowest part on the south, east, and west, the small houses of the peasants.
Yagul has complexes in which the rooms multiply by the tens until they seem a labyrinth, like that of the Palace of the Six Patios.

The Pyramid of the Niches in El Tajín, Veracruz; it was constructed of slender slabs of stone, fitted without mortar, which made the delicate design possible.

Traditional Indian dances survive in many regions of Mexico, including Oaxaca, Veracruz and Puebla. The dance of the Quetzalines, executed in the archaeological zone of El Tajín.

EL TAJIN

Surrounded by a landscape where the exuberant vegetation symbolizes the power of nature, the artists of El Tajín incorporated it in their reliefs, creating a distinctive style that can best be seen in the panels of the pelota court. The city was the most important center, for six centuries, of the northern Gulf Coast. Contacts were maintained with Teotihuacán, with which it was contemporary, as well as with the Maya area, as can still be seen in the Maya vault of Building A in El Tajín Chico. The masterpiece of the architectural style of this culture is the creative Pyramid of the Niches.

LA VENTA

On the Gulf Coast, the city of La Venta, Tabasco, capital of the enigmatic and first civilization of America, has greatly deteriorated because of the material used in the constructions: beaten earth and sand. This is why the sculpture was transferred to the Museum Park built in Villahermosa, the capital of the state, where it can be better protected.
After the year 1000 B.C. the Olmecs of La Venta created some of the most beautiful and impressive sculpture on the continent with basalt that was quarried and transported from 100 km. away.

Above: Colossal Head No. 1 from La Venta.

Right: Altar No. 4 from La Venta. The niche symbolizes the mouth of the jaguar.

PALENQUE

Outstanding among all the Maya sites, it is the loveliest, with an art of great refinement, due in particular to the use a ductile material, stucco, which covers all the walls. Set at the foot of a chain of hills covered by an exuberant tropical vegetation, which serves as backdrop for the white buildings, it lies opposite prairies of a less intense green which extend to the horizon.

Of all the centers of the entire early classic period of the Maya culture (A.D. 300-600), the architectural style of Palenque has distinctive features, foundations with inclined and plain elements, small temples on top with a sanctuary inside containing beautiful sculptures dedicated to the gods or the symbols of the cult to which they were consecrated.

The Palenque style is reflected in the type of roof, present only at this site, as well as in the tall and elegant pierced

cresting, decorated with reliefs in stucco, false facades that crowned the real facade and are known as flying or airborn facades and which rivalled the tall trees in the background. Inside the sanctuaries are fine panels with various religious motifs such as the three in the Temple of the Sun, the Temple of the Cross — in the Museo Nacional de Antropología — and in that of the Foliated Cross. Inside the Temple of the Beautiful Relief is a carved panel with a person on a throne; here the religious has been abandoned in favor of a political theme.

Palenque; at the back, the Temple of the Inscriptions, on the right, the Palace, and on the left, the Temple of the Sun.

The Palace is the result of various periods of
construction in which long corridors with dwellings for
the governors and Maya priests were superposed.

Right: the Tower of the Palace; it is a unique
feature in Maya architecture.

THE PALACE

Covered corridors and dwellings with high vaults which
were someimes decorated with niches in strange shapes
stand on an enormous platform 300 m wide and 240
deep. Various internal courtyards provide the rooms with
light and space; furthermore, they form units of inter-
related decorative motifs, carved in stucco and covering
the pillars which support the typical Palenque roofs; in
some cases, panels in a soft smooth stone that permitted
the artist to execute all his designs with great skill.

The Tower, a unique structure in Meso-America, seems
to have been used as an observatory. In the patio where
the tower stands are sanitary installations with drains
which led to the city aqueduct.

The typical roof that all the buildings have seems to have
been designed to provide protection from the rain both
for the wooden lintels of the doors as well as for the stucco reliefs and, probably, also the personages who walked
along the broad corridors.

Above: one of the inner patios of the Palace.

Left: the typical Mayan roofing system allowed sufficiently high but narrow spaces, decorated with niches.

Above, right: stucco was used by the artists of Palenque to express a refined sensitivity, as shown in this relief on one flank of the Palace.

Right: the Maya vault is the reproduction in stone of the roof of the peasant huts, helping to preserve the buildings.

Above, left: east patio of House C of the Palace.

Below, left: the figures carved in the patio of House C, may represent captives or slaves.

The Temple of the Inscriptions contains glyphs inside which have not been completely deciphered.

THE TEMPLE OF THE INSCRIPTIONS

The building was erected in 692 after the sarcophagus had been fashioned and the crypt built. Three phases of construction can be easily identified: in the first, eight stepped levels with a narrow staircase; in the second and third three taller tiers were added, sort of buttresses, with a broader staircase; solely the base was involved without touching the temple on the upper part.

The temple has a portico with five entrances and stucco figures on the pillars that form it: priests holding small children in their arms.

The temple takes its name from the 620 hieroglyphics carved on panels on the walls of the portico and inside. Cresting, of which little remains, crowns the roof.

After various seasons of work, a staircase was found in the inner room, entirely filled with earth and rubble to block off the way. After excavating, a triangular stone sealing off the entrance was uncovered; opposite were the remains of five youths who had been sacrificed and various objects that accompanied them.

When the stone which covered the entrance was removed, the lamps illuminated a crypt 9 m. wide and 4 deep, terminating in a Maya vault 7 m. high and reinforced by heavy beams. Filling almost the entire crypt was an enormous monolithic sarcophagus, resting on six stone supports, and covered by an enormous slab weighing 8 tons

In the excavations of 1952 a staircase 22 m. long was discovered in the Temple of the Inscriptions. It was filled with earth and rubble to block off access to the tomb.

Side view of the Temple of the Inscriptions, permitting the construction of the pyramid over the crypt to be appreciated.

The monolithic sarcophagus and the limestone slab which covered it, weighing eight tons.

Inside the sarcophagus, covered with a richly carved slab, a personage decked in jade jewels and covered with a red dust that symbolized life had been laid. The Nine Lords of the world of the dead were carved on the walls of the crypt.

In Palenque, the Temple of the Sun is a fine example of how cresting can become an airborn facade, lending the monument an airiness not to be found in the other Maya sites.

Palenque was built with the tall tropical forest as a backdrop.

and finely carved with an elegant figure, lying on his back, accompanied by elements related to the corn plant and other fertility symbols.

Inside the sarcophagus was the skeleton of a man 40 or 50 years old, 1.73 m. tall, richly covered with jewels of jade, and other objects. His breast was almost completely hidden by an enormous pectoral, made of strings of jade beads, which also covered his wrists and ankles. On his head rested a diadem in the same material and he had rings of jade strung into several locks of hair as well as on all his fingers.

His face was covered with a mask made of pieces of jade and his ears were adorned with the same stone and a pearl.

But the man buried here was not alone; on the walls of the crypt were sculptured nine personages in procession, who have been interpreted as the Nine Lords of the night and the world of the dead. On the sides of the sarcophagus a row of persons was also carved, possibly ancestors who accompanied him in his last journey.

Many of the offerings in the tomb were dedicated to the continuation of life in the other world: the jade and cinnabar beads, a red dust which completely covered the body of the dead man.

In no other part of America is there a tomb like this: its importance is both artistic and historical. The personage, probably a governor-priest, was buried with a luxury and an ostentation to be equalled solely in ancient Egypt.

NORTH GROUP

Throughout the various periods five buildings were built on a platform. They comprised a portico, sanctuary and rooms at the sides, decorated with reliefs in stucco and crowned with cresting. The Temple of the Chief, situated to one side of the group, is similar in structure with the exception of three small tombs found underneath the floor of the porch, in which offerings of jade, shell and bone were found.

Palenque is, without doubt, one of the major examples of Maya art.

THE YUCATAN PENINSULA

At present the Yucatán peninsula is divided into three states of the Republic of Mexico: Yucatán, Campeche and Quintana Roo, in which around 450,000 Maya-speaking peoples live.

Its present political division does not in the least correspond to the boundaries of the pre-Columbian period, for the development throughout the peninsula was not uniform. It is solely in the archaeological remains that different regional art styles are manifested and distinct characteristics are to be found in the following areas: the northeast with sites such as Tulum and Coba; the north, with sites such as Chichén Itzá; the region around the small mountain ridges in what are now the states of Yucatán and Campeche, and, further south, the centers with styles of their own such as the Chenes or the Río Bec, that reveal greater contact with the Maya groups outside the peninsula.

The peninsula of Yucatán was the first place the Spaniards described when they sent expeditions from the island of Cuba in the 16th century; the first Europeans arrived here and lived together with the Indians, and it was here that the first mestizos appeared when children were born to Gonzalo Guerrero who had been shipwrecked and remade his life among the Maya, marrying the daughter of the Chetumal chief and adapting to the Indian customs.

Merida was founded in 1542, the Yucatán peninsula maintaining a certain independence from the rest of Mexico, in its historical development, since the final submission of the natives to the Spaniards did not take place until 1546. From then on the Indians were gradually subjugated, which led to a reaction on their part, and in 1847 they rebelled against those who were not Mayans, which resulted in a bloody war called the War of Castes, in which various aspects related to pre-Columbian cults came to the fore. In the end they were defeated in 1849.

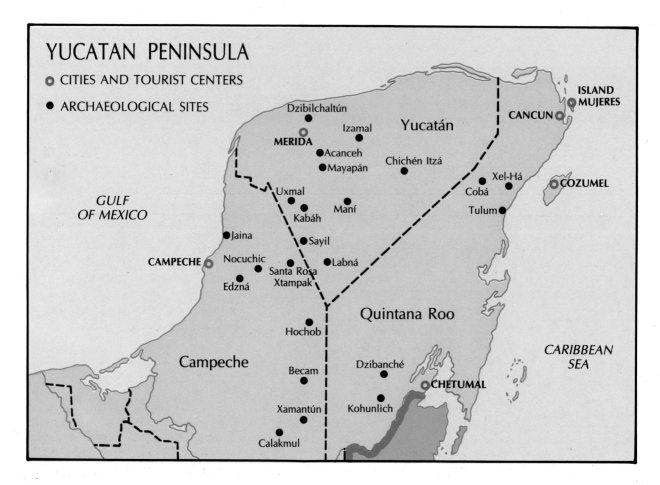

Above: the entry to the Palace of the Governor
in Uxmal, Yucatán, as it is now.

Right: lithograph by F. Catherwood published in
London in 1844; it was taken directly from the rough
sketches the English draftsman made on the spot
of the Maya arch that stands at the entrance
to the Palace of the Governor in Uxmal.

MUSEO REGIONAL DE MERIDA

Right: the Lord of Kabáh, sculpture with Toltec features.

Below: the Cantón Palace, first a private home, then the house of the Governor of the state of Yucatán, and at present, Museo Regional de Merida.

Opposite, above left: this divinity, with a deformed leg, has been interpreted as a possible Tezcatlipoca.

Opposite, above right: ceremonial urn.

Opposite, below: the meaning of the sculptures of Chac-Mool, a reclining figure, executed at the beginning of the Toltec culture (950 A.D.), continues to be an enigma.

LOS PORTAESTANDARTES ERAN...
PARA SOSTENER LAS ASTAS O M...
SUPERIOR COLGABAN BANDERAS...
GENERALMENTE ESTAS ESTATU...
UNA FINA CAPA DE ESTUCO SOB...
DIVERSOS COLORES SEGÚN EL O...
RESALTAR.

ALGUNOS PORTAESTANDARTES T...
INCRUSTACIONES DE HUESO, CO...
MARCAR MEJOR CIERTOS RASGO...
CHICHÉN ITZÁ.

OTRAS A LA TERCERA, ÉSTAS SE COLOCAN EN PLATO SOBRE EL...
ABDOMEN. LOS MAYAS PENSABAN QUE PUDIERON SERVIR PARA...
DEPOSITAR LAS OFRENDAS DE LOS FIELES.

SUS MÁS GRANDES MÓDULOS PRODUCES INTERMEDIARIOS ENTRE...
LOS MEXICANOS Y LO DIVINO. LLEGABAN ENTRE LAS COSTAS DE...
SE ENCIMA Y SE HIZO SU PARA REPRESENTAR A LOS DIOS FEAS...
JAAR DI MARIOS Y MÁS. TARDE EN MAYA GENERAS DE QUE...
ESTAS ESTATUAS ESTUVIERON PINTADAS CON VARIOS...
COLORES.

SE HAN HALLADO ESCULTURAS SIMILARES EN LA COSTA...
CENTRAL DE QUINTANA ROO, EN TULA, HGO; SO, EN...
TENAYUACAN, MICHOACÁN, Y EN EL DISTRITO FEDERAL...
ENTRE LOS RUINAS DE LA ANTIGUA TENOCHTITLAN.

EDZNA

Situated in the central-western area of the Yucatán peninsula, Edzná is contemporary with other cities of the classic period, such as Palenque and Yaxchilán, and therefore maintained contacts with some of the classic sites in the south. This is corroborated by the presence of at least twenty steles with calendar dates that were made between the years 670 and 810. The Puuc style seems to have begun in some of its buildings and the best example is the Main Pyramid or Templo Mayor. A tall construction of five tiers in which various functions were combined rises up opposite a large plaza. At the top is a temple with high coping, set on four tiers.

The facade is of great simplicity, ornamented here and there with elements which recall the Puuc style, such as the columns which separate the entrances of the fourth level.

The Nunnery Quadrangle in Uxmal. It was called the House of the Nuns (Casa de las Monjas) by the Spaniards because they thought it was a convent.

In the foreground, the Pelota Court, on the right,
the Pyramid of the Soothsayer, and at the back,
the Nunnery Quadrangle.

UXMAL

Antonio de Ciudad Real, a Spanish Franciscan friar who visited Uxmal in 1588, left a detailed description of the structures here, commenting that not even the Indians themselves knew who built them or when.

According to the books of Chilam Balam de Chumayel, manuscripts written in the Maya tongue but with Latin characters, and the writings of Alfonso Ponce, a Franciscan who visited the site in the 16th century, the city of Uxmal was founded in the middle of the 7th century A.D. In the 10th century the Xiues arrived from the Central Plateau and occupied Uxmal, imposing the worship of Tláloc and of Quetzalcóatl, « feathered serpent ». In its early period the cult of Chac, god of rain, was very important in Uxmal. Since the Puuc region is situated in an arid dry zone, cisterns and « *chultunes* » were built to retain water.

This cult to Chac is substantiated by the great number of masks representing the god which are found on the buildings in Uxmal, as well as in other Maya cities in the area. Uxmal lies near a row of hills known by the name of Puuc, which in Maya language means « mountain ridge », a name later given to the architectural style characteristic of the sites in this region, and of which the best examples are in Uxmal. There are fifteen groups of buildings, distributed from north to south, over an area approximately two-kilometer long.

One of the features of the Puuc style is a molding that runs all along the building, called « cord molding » which reproduces in stone the rope fastenings used to secure the walls of the Maya huts. The rows of small columns to be found both in the frieze and the base of the buildings constitute another decorative element.

Patterns of geometric elements, repeated ad infinitum, were made with pieces of cut and decorated stone. The presence of the serpent in the decoration is a sign of external influence; it was never, in any case, as obvious as at Chichén Itzá.

PYRAMID OF THE SOOTHSAYER

The form of this building was quite unusual: the elliptical plan was the result of various periods of construction, with five temples at different levels and in different styles.

It is also known as the Pyramid of the Dwarf or of the Wizard for a legend recounts that it was built by the son of a witch, born from an egg.

A sculpture called the Queen of Uxmal, which may personify the god Kukulkán, was found in the first temple.

The northwest side of the Pyramid of the Soothsayer, with remains of the first temple covered by later structures.

West staircase of the Pyramid of the Soothsayer, decorated on both sides with masks of Chac, the god of rain.

NUNNERY QUADRANGLE

This large complex, one of the most important in Uxmal, is built on a vast platform, around which are four structures, each one decorated in a different way. The building on the north is taller than the rest, has a staircase with a stele at the center, and a small temple on either side. Chac masks, meanders, « huts », entwined serpents and geometric motifs, all decorative elements of the Puuc style profusely adorn the facades.

Above, left: rear part of the Eastern Building of the Nunnery Quadrangle.

Below, left: the patio of the Quadrangle with the altar at the center; on the right, the Temple of Venus.

Right: the Maya artist obtained extraordinary effects through his use of stone and the play of light.

Below: detail of the frieze of the West Building of the Nunnery Quadrangle, decorated with serpents, decorative theme that predominated in some of the buildings in Uxmal.

The importance the Mayas attributed to rain is proved by the great number of representations of the god Chac which decorate the Maya monuments. Mask on the North Building of the Nunnery Quadrangle.

Below: the horizontal proportions of the buildings of the Nunnery Quadrangle accentuate the decoration on the upper part; North Building and the temple of Venus.

Above, right: the East Building of the Quadrangle differs in its decoration from the other three buildings; the Pyramid of the Soothsayer rises up in the back.

Below, right: detail of the East Building. The facade centers around the central doorway which is broader than the others and surmounted by a different decoration.

A section of the Palace of the Governor.

Above, far left: masks of the god Chac, each comprised of 18 pieces of stone cut and carved to fit perfectly.

PALACE OF THE GOVERNOR

This fine building stands on a large platform. Its proportions and decoration make it one of the best examples of the architecture of Uxmal. The arches which separate the facade into three sectors are also noteworthy.
Opposite the palace staircase stands the original and strange sculpture of two felines, joined at the breast, with the head of one turned north and of the other south.

Above, far right: decoration of the corner of the Palace of the Governor. The masks are accompanied by fretwork and serpents.

Below, right: view of the facade of the Palace of the Governor with its arches, a solution escogitated by the Mayas to unite buildings that were originally separate. In the foreground, the statue which represents two jaguars joined at the breast.

Above, left: the Great Pyramid, southwest of the Palace of the Governor, and at one side the Palomar, so-called due to the singular design of its cresting.

Above, right: the Pelota Court in Uxmal, which makes it possible to see the system of construction used by the Mayas; the filler of earth and uncut stone was faced with perfectly cut and polished blocks.

Below, left: the House of the Turtles; the cornice was decorated with finely carved small turtles.

The ring hewn in stone of the Pelota Court has inscriptions of dates; presumably the players had to throw a solid rubber ball through the center.

Above: the Codz-Poop of Kabáh covered
with Chac masks.

*Left: blocks of stone form the features
of the god Chac.*

Above, right: the Great Palace of Kabáh.

Below, right: the Arch of Kabáh.

KABAH

Situated 15 km. from Uxmal it is joined to it by a cause-
way that begins with a plain stone arch. During the 9th
and 10th centuries it was the second largest city in the
north of the Yucatán peninsula.
It is comprised of a series of large-scale buildings of extraordinary architectural quality, most of them built in
Puuc style.
The most striking building here is called Codz-Poop,
which means « rolled mat », referring to the shape that
depicts the curve of the nose of the god Chac.
The entire facade was covered with masks of the god,
from the ground up to the roof, endless repetitions of the
strange image which strike us as extraordinarily beautiful.

The Great Palace of Sayil, built in the Puuc style.

Recollections of the building techniques employed in the Maya huts: the small columns with three collars.

SAYIL

In an area of low mountain vegetation in the Maya region stands Sayil.

Some of the buildings, scattered over a wide area, are magnificent examples of the Maya architecture of this region. The Great Palace has three stories, the first of which serves as terrace for the second, but with a different decor. The former is very simple but, for the first time, there is a difference in the decoration of each side of the stairs. The second level has the most important decoration, consisting of small columns with three col-

The ground floor of the ample buildings served as dwellings for the governors and priests.

Mask on a corner of the Great Palace of Sayil, representing the open maw of a serpent.

lars. The doorway consists of simple columns, with a solitary capital (disengaged), which lend a sober elegant air to the entire building. At this same level the wall frieze contains the masks that are so frequent in the centers of this region, together with other exceedingly rare motifs, including a reptile which is repeated in various occasions, accompanied by a part of the body of the Descending god, which relates Sayil to sites such as Tulum and Coba. Sayil presents us with noteworthy examples of the Puuc style of architecture, the culmination of a broad development which was perfected in the working of stone, and of which the best examples date to the 7th-8th centuries A.D.

LABNA

This ancient city consists of various building complexes. Of particular note are some of the palaces and temples, such as the one called the « Mirador ». But the most beautiful and characteristic of all is the Arch of Labná. In its form and in the decoration on its main facade, it is one of the best examples of Maya architecture.

DZIBILCHALTUN

Various isolated building complexes which communicate with each other characterize this site. The best known is the Group of the Seven « Muñecas »: a large platform with seven constructions on top. The first, with its recessed corners, recalls the Maya constructions of the Guatemalan region of Petén.

Above, left: the Arch of Labná is a masterpiece of this type of architecture.

Below, left: F. Catherwood drew the Arch of Labná as he saw it in one of his trips to Yucatán.

Right: the Castillo of Labná.

Below: Temple of the Group of the Seven Muñecas of Dzibilchaltún.

The grottos of Balancanchén preserve offerings to the gods of the netherworld.

Right: grottos of Bolonchén in a drawing by F. Catherwood, made on the spot in 1841.

CAVES IN THE YUCATAN PENINSULA

The lowlands of the Maya region are formed of calcareous earth with subterranean caverns. Running or stagnant water is to be found in this soil. As time passed these caves eroded and some of the stone gave way, so that formed cisterns or wells for water called *cenotes*.

For a thousand years the Mayas of the north of the peninsula explored all the caves they could discover, in the hopes of finding water. In them they deposited a great quantity of offerings for the god Chac.

Even though the caves of Bolonchén lie at a great depth, Maya man reached the bottom in his anxious search for survival. In those of Balancanchén, between Mérida and Chichén Itzá, the offerings of the Mayas have been preserved just there where they were discovered.

Presumably the grotto of Loltun contains the remains of the first inhabitants of the Yucatán peninsula.

CHICHÉN ITZÁ

Between 700 and 900 A.D. all of Meso-America was subjected to a series of transformations which manifested themselves in the various art styles and in all aspects of society.

There are pre-Columbian legends which tell how various groups abandoned the cities and the centers of the classic period to emigrate to distant lands. Some of these groups were directly connected with the god Quetzalcóatl; others, with the chief Ce Acatl Topiltzin Quetzalcóatl, the builder of Tula. Undoubtedly they were frequently fused into a single figure, since Ce Acatl Topiltzin Quetzalcóatl bore the name of the god whose priest he was. According to the Maya historical sources, Quetzalcóatl arrived in the Maya area and named himself Kukulkán (Kukul: bird and Kan: serpent). His arrival brought a series of changes in diverse aspects of Maya life: art styles, representations of the gods, government, military and economical organization. All this is known as the Maya-Toltec period.

In studying the similarities between Tula and Chichén Itzá — such as the buildings of the Temple of Tlahuizcalpantecutli (Tula) and that of the Warriors (Chichén Itzá) — the logical explanation seemed to be that Tula influenced Chichén Itzá. Recently some archaeologists think that it may have been the other way around and this idea seems to be confirmed by the recent discoveries of the paintings of Cacaxtla, Tlaxcala, a place closer to Tula than to Chichén Itzá.

In the north of the Maya area the Indians, using the Castilian alphabet, described their traditions, ritual myths, prophecies and chronologies in what are called the Books of Chilam Balam, or « the books of the soothsayer of occult things », for the Chilán or Chilam were priests of a specific type, dedicated to oracles and prophecies, and doubtless also experts in the history of the area. Some of these books bear the name of the peoples who were involved such as the Chilam Balam de Maní or the Chilam Balam de Tizimín, Chumayel, and still others. In addition to these historical sources, we have a highly estimable work, written in 1566 by the bishop of Yucatán, Diego de Landa, who recorded in his book « Relación de las cosas de Yucatán » a whole series of historical, religious and calendar data furnished him by the Maya Indians of his time.

The Chilam Balam de Chumayel recounts that the Itzáes had the same origins as the Xiues, relating them also to the Putunes or Maya-Chontales, trader-sailors who controlled the coasts of the Yucatán peninsula. A first group arrived in A.D. 918, conquering Chichén and building the substructure of the Castillo, painting frescoes with battle scenes and contributing various new cultural elements. Later, in 970, another group arrived with a greater quantity of Toltec characteristics; they built the Temple of the Warriors, the Castillo and the Pelota Court and

Above, left: the Castillo of Chichén Itzá as its was in the 19th century when F. Catherwood drew it.

Above: the Castillo as it is now, after reconstruction has restored its original appearance.

developed metalwork.

In order to maintain control of the area recently conquered, the Itzáes allied themselves to some of the lords who governed the neighboring cities such as Uxmal, Mayapán and Izamal, with whom they maintained strong ties and the same cult of Kukulkán — an alliance known as the League of Mayapán. The result was the dominion of a territory in which the same religion was practised, with allied governors to control the tributes and trade.

Later, Mayapán conquered Chichén Itzá, from 1185 to 1400, and it remained under the dominion of the Cocomes.

The city of Chichén Itzá was first settled towards the south, around the Xtoloc *cenote*, which supplied drinking water, and various groups of ceremonial buildings were built in the Chenes and Puuc styles. In the former the decoration covers the entire facade, while the latter concentrates on the friezes in the upper part of the building. But all of them were made using mosaics of stone that was perfectly cut, polished, wrought and assembled to form the decoration, whether this consisted of Chac masks or of fretwork in a geometric style, accompanied by small columns, tamborcillas and columns supporting the roof of the entrance.

The Chenes style developed in the region of the state of Campeche with influences from Edzná and Río Bec, which flourished in the southern part of the Maya area. The name of those who lived in Chichén Itzá during the classic period (7th-9th cent.) and constructed the first ceremonial center in the environs of the Xtoloc *cenote* is not known, but they were not Itzáes. The buildings display architectural characteristics which correspond to the Puuc or Chenes style, and these include the Akab-Dzib, Las Monjas, the Annex of Las Monjas, the Iglesia, the Chichánchob, the House of the Deer (Venado), the Three Lintels, and still others.

THE CASTILLO

This pyramid with nine tiers measures 60 m. per side and is 24 m. high, with a staircase on each side and a temple on the top.

The Castillo has two structures which correspond to two different periods; the oldest is totally covered by the later. The decorative motifs on the facade are serpents and tigers which indicate a Toltec influence.

The statue of a Chac-Mool was discovered in the temple found in the substructure, and, in the sanctuary raised on the upper part of the pyramid, another one of a jaguar

Left: the throne in the form of a jaguar, painted red and encrusted with jade, in the inner temple of the Castillo.

Below, left: the heads of the feathered serpents, on either side of the staircases of the Castillo, represent the god Kukulkán.

Right: a warrior carved into the entrance jamb of the temple of the Castillo.

Below: serpent columns revealing a strong Toltec influence at the entrance to the temple of the Castillo.

Above: the building of the Temple of the Warriors
with the columns forming the vestibule, in front, and
on the right, the Group of the Thousand Columns.

Left: the warriors carved in the pillars are one of the
principal themes in Chichén Itzá; their rich attire
indicates their social position.

Right: the entrance to the Temple of the Warriors
displays some of the principal elements of the Maya-
Toltec architecture: a « Chac-Mool » figure, serpent
columns, and pillars with carved warriors.

painted red and incrusted with jade, which probably
served as a throne.
This temple is composed of two independent units. The
principal entrance, with two serpent columns similar to
those found in Tula, leads to an antechamber, and in the
part behind, to the sanctuary, which has two pillars decorated with bas-reliefs.
The temple terminates in a series of snail-shaped merlons.
Figures of warriors appear in the bas-reliefs. Its
monumentality and decoration make it the most impressive building in all of Chichén Itzá.

Motifs which represent the gods Chac and Kukulkán-Quetzalcóatl are found on the side walls and the corners of the Temple of the Warriors.

Other Maya-Toltec elements in the Temple of the Warriors: a standard-bearer and the lateral termination of the staircase in the form of a serpent.

TEMPLE OF THE WARRIORS

This building is the one which most resembles the Toltec structures, especially the Temple of Tlahuizcalpantecutli in Tula. It rises on a square base and its stepped tiers are composed of *talud* and a slender *tablero* cornice, decorated with warriors, eagles and jaguars devouring human hearts, accompanied by the figure of Kukulkán. The upper part of the temple consists of two large rooms. The first has a doorway with three openings separated by fine serpent pillars; inside are twelve pillars with bas-reliefs of gods, warriors, and Kukulkán, which support the vault of the ceiling. The second room, or sanctuary, has eight pillars which support a flat ceiling; in the back is a stone altar, set on small atlantes figures.

Right: the god Kukulkán, depicted as in Tula in the form of a man-bird-serpent with a large feather headdress.

Below: the stone altar that stands at the back of the Temple of the Warriors. The sculptures representing small atlantes are very frequent in Chichén Itzá.

The external walls of the temple are built with a *talud* that is completely bare below, and with a vertical wall where the decorative motifs include Maya elements such as masks of the god Chac, and Toltec elements such as representations of Kukulkán emerging from the maw of a feathered serpent. Between the staircase and the entrance the sculpture of a Chac-Mool rises up and two standard-bearers, an element widely diffused in the architecture of the central Plateau, first in Tula and later among the Mexicas or Aztecs.

Inside this building is a substructure which displays almost the same architectural elements, on a smaller scale.

The Temple of the Warriors is part of the Group of the Thousand Columns.

Row of columns in the northwest of the Group of the Thousand Columns. Each column consists of five drums terminating in a simple square capital.

Right: the entrance to the Temple of the Warriors is marked by two columns in the form of rattlesnakes, with the head forming the base and the rattles, the capital.

Above, left: the Platform of Venus is square in plan and has staircases on all four sides. It is known also as the « tomb of the Chac-Mool » since a statue of this type was found inside. The Mayas may have presented various pageants here.

In its reliefs, the Platform of the Eagles and Jaguars has eagles devouring human hearts.

Left: a detail of the decoration of the Platform of Venus: the sign of the first month of the year, the representation of Kukulkán, and different Maya allegories of the planet Venus.

PLATFORM OF THE EAGLES AND THE TZOMPANTLI

The Platform of the Eagles and the Tzompantli are other buildings which clearly demonstrate the influence of Tula in Chichén Itzá. There are many elements which unite these two cities in a common religious expression, notwithstanding the fact that the quality of work in stone might be superior in the Maya area.

Chichén Itzá was a great trading center which controlled raw materials and regional products, as well as the craft production.

Monetary units such as colored shells, blankets, copper bells, tongs and hatchets, jade beads, quetzal feathers, hides and cocoa pods, served for commercial transactions. During the occupation by the Itzáes metallurgy was introduced, which reveals relations with various sites in Central America. Objects in gold, copper, copper with tin, copper with lead and silver were recovered from the Sacred *Cenote* or the well of the Sacrifices; some of these were objects worn by the victims thrown alive into the waters of the *Cenote* in homage to the gods.

Above, left: the stone platform that calls to mind the human sacrifices, according to the warrior-religious mysticism, is covered with reliefs of skulls and resembles a structure that is typical of central Mexico called Tzompantli.

Below, left: detail of the Altar of Skulls, whose purpose may have been that of displaying a series of stands with the skulls of the victims.

Above: the Annex of the Temple of the Jaguars in the rear of the Pelota Court.

Right: a throne in the form of a jaguar, at the entrance to the Annex of the Temple of the Jaguars.

THE PELOTA COURT

On the west side of the large plaza on which the Castillo faces was built one of the various pelota courts to be found in Chichén Itzá. In this case however it is one that displays Toltec features. It is the largest court known in all of Mexico.

The benches to be found on either side of the grounds are decorated with bas-reliefs; some of them have been as useful in explaining the meaning of the game as they were in showing the close relationship with the Mexican Gulf Coast. These reliefs tell us of the close bonds that existed between the game, human sacrifice by decapitation, and fertility rites, a basic concept in the representations of Meso-American religion.

Left: the ring of the Pelota Court of Chichén Itzá.

Below: the bench of the Pelota Court; the relief in the center depicts the symbol of death and the decapitation of one of the players; blood drips from his neck, symbolized by a bundle of serpents, since the game was related to mythical and religious motives.

Above, right: the Pelota Court with its grounds 150 meters long, is the largest in Chichén Itzá and in pre-Columbian Mexico. In the foreground, the Temple of the Jaguars and in the back, the Temple of the North.

Below, right: the Temple of the North or of the Bearded Man, is decorated with birds, trees and flowers, and with the head of a bearded man.

The Cenote Sagrado or of the Sacrifices was used
exclusively for ceremonies. Offerings in gold, copal
and pottery were recovered from the bottom,
as well as the remains of victims.

CHICHANCHOB

This building is known as Chichánchob, « small holes », and as the Casa Colorada (Red House), due to the border painted in red on the wall of the portico.

The temple consists of a vestibule with three entrances and, at the back, three rooms. The facade is extremely simple: smooth walls and with only two moldings and two crestings on the upper part. The oldest part is in the center; later another one with Chac masks was built more to the front. Inside the building is a date of the year 850.

The destruction of the archaeological buildings is due as much to the passage of time as to the cupidity of the looters.

Below: the Casa Colorada, « Chichánchob », corresponds to the oldest constructions of Chichén Itzá, as demonstrated by its style, prior to the Maya-Toltec.

Above: the stars were studied in buildings such as the Observatory or Caracol.

Left: the tower of the Observatory.

THE CARACOL OR ASTRONOMICAL OBSERVATORY

The Mayas knew the positions of the stars and studied their movements. For this scope they raised structures such as the Observatory of Chichén Itzá, considered transitional between the Maya and the Toltec styles.
The Caracol was built on a large rectangular platform

Above: side view of the Observatory.

Right: one of the entrances to the
tower of the Observatory.

and, like so many of the pre-Columbian buildings, is the
result of various superpositions that modified diverse
parts of the structure. In its center the large platform has
a circular tower, which was later enlarged, and a base was
built which appeared to support it but actually only surrounded it. The name of this 13-meter high structure
comes from the winding staircase (caracol: snail) inside
which leads to an upper room for astronomical observa-
tion.

Left: bas-reliefs in the Temple of the Tableros Esculpidos.

Below: a simple Maya arch in the same temple.

Above, right: part of the great Complex of Las Monjas in Chichén Itzá.

Right: rear view of the first Temple of Las Monjas.

Above, left: the arched enclosure called the Iglesia.

Left: rear view of the Iglesia.

Above: the fine facade of the Annex of Las Monjas.

Right: masks of the god of rain decorate the Annex of Las Monjas and the frieze of the Iglesia.

THE IGLESIA

Near the Complex of Las Monjas stands the Iglesia, which owes its name to the fact that it was so close to what the Spaniards considered the dwellings of the Maya priestesses, and which they called Las Monjas. The building has a single room, rectangular in plan, and makes a good contrast with the Annex. The lower part of the walls is bare and decoration is limited to the upper part, where projecting Chac masks are framed by two heavy cornice moldings.

The cresting bears the same fretwork motif and large masks of the same god. The Iglesia, together with the Annex of Las Monjas, comprises a fine complex which dates back to the 7th and 8th centuries A.D.

Above, left: the Casa Colorada, the Ossuary, the House of the Deer and the Observatory.

The Mercado, a portico with two parallel galleries, in which the columns acquire classic proportions.

Left: the Akab-Dzib, one of the oldest buildings in Chichén Itzá.

CASA DE LAS MONJAS (Nunnery)

The result of various superpositions, various separate buildings existed in the first period: Las Monjas, the East Annex and the Southeast Annex, all with double rooms crowned by cresting. Later a larger building was constructed which was superposed on Las Monjas and on part of the East Annex. The first building had a decoration of fretwork all over the wall, while the second is much simpler. The lintels of the first building bear hieroglyphic inscriptions.

The eastern facade of the Annex of Las Monjas, a building with a ground floor composed of several rooms, is completely covered with masks of the god Chac, a magnificent example of the Chenes style. The internal wall of this building has Chac masks from the ground up to the molding.

The frieze is also completely covered by Chac masks, with a seated personage in the center, adorned with a great feather headdress.

The fangs of the god appear on the upper part of the doorway, equivalating the entrance to the open mouth of this god. In its proportions and the exuberance of the decoration the entire complex strikes one for its great beauty.

AKAB-DZIB

It is comprised of a central building with one at either side, and with eighteen rooms covered with Maya vaults. The aspect is of great simplicity and the facade is composed of a smooth wall with two moldings in the upper part and crowned with cresting. On the lintel of one of the inner rooms there are various glyphs, undeciphered, after which the building is named — Akab-Dzib or « obscure writing ».

COBA

Situated between two large lakes and with a network of artificially constructed roadways, Cobá was the oldest and most important Maya city in the northeast of Yucatán.

It has a large number of steles, with calendar dates which tell of its creation in the year 600 A.D. up until the 15th century.

The Mayas built many large-size monuments, such as the Nohoch Mul, taller than the Castillo of Chichén Itzá, and Structure 38, where one of the vaults covers an internal space of almost four meters.

Left: Building 1 of Coba.

Below: Stele 20 of the Nohoch Mul Group.

Above, right: Structure 1 of Nohoch Mul.

Below, right: the column in the center comes from the Puuc style.

The buildings of Tulum are set between the Great Wall and the Mexican Caribbean sea.

TULUM

When the Spaniards sent various expeditions from the island of Cuba to discover new territories in 1518, Juan de Grijalva, in his excursion along the coast of the Yucatán peninsula, saw a town « as large as Seville », with a tower taller than he had ever seen. The site mentioned seems to have been Tulum, then called Zama, and the tower must have been the highest until the one called Castillo was built.

Tulum was one of the most important centers on the east coast of the Yucatán peninsula, and even if the period of greatest importance was in the postclassic of the Maya culture (1200-1400), there are records of earlier dates (A.D. 564) on steles.

At the front and on either side of the site is a wall four m. high, essential for its defense, since the Maya groups were not politically stable.

Within the ramparts are the principal buildings as well as various roads which put them in communication; but there were also others outside which reached southwards. The city of Tulum has an architectural style which combines elements of different regions and periods: the Maya vault coexists with flat roofs, the small sanctuaries and stucco sculptures with porticoes formed of pillars in masonry, faced with stucco or serpent-shaped in Toltec style. The buildings have bare walls with friezes on the upper part, accompanied by molding and masks on the corners.

The Maya sailors and traders landed in the cove of Tulum, next to the building of the Castillo, to trade their products.

When F. Catherwood visited Tulum in 1842, he drew the Castillo, and later reconstructions were in part based on this evidence.

THE CASTILLO

The principal structure is the Castillo, the tallest building on the site, whose present form is the result of various periods of construction. On the upper part the broad entrance is composed of two serpent columns which divide it into three. Above, interrupting the frieze, are three niches occupied by figures in stucco: the central one, by the Descending god, who was frequently represented in Tulum.

Above, right: the Castillo, the highest building in Tulum, faces inland. Its appearance left a deep impression on the early Spanish navigators who arrived on the coasts of the Yucatán peninsula.

Right: crossing the ramparts through the western entry makes it possible to appreciate the complex of the most important monuments, with leaning walls, and cornices on the upper part.

TEMPLE OF THE FRESCOES

Also called Structure 16, it is to be found opposite the Castillo. The main entrance has four columns, and the decoration is composed of a niche on the front with the figure of the Descending god and masks on the corners, possibly of the god Kukulkán.

Inside, the figures in the wall paintings have been identified as the rain god Chac and various female divinities associated with rites related to vegetation and animals: serpents, lizards, fish, and other marine elements.

In one of these paintings, with a black ground, the goddess Ix Chel is accompanied by the god Chac. This goddess is represented as an old woman, wife of Itzamná, lord of the sky; he is identified with the sun and she with the moon.

The flank of the Temple of the Frescoes, with masks on the corners; the interior is decorated with murals.

Stucco figures adorn the niches of the upper part of the Temple of the Frescoes.

Above, right: one of the simple buildings in the complex of the Castillo.

Right: Ix Chel, « Lady of the rainbow », oddess of medicine, of birth and eaving, on a black ground, accompanied y two representations of the god Chac, n the Temple of the Frescoes.

Above, left: the House of Chultun or Structure 20.

Above: sketch of the same Structure 20, made on the pot by F. Catherwood.

Below, left: the House of the Column or Structure 21; it may have been the largest building in Tulum.

The style of the paintings in Tulum denotes the influence of the Mixtec codexes of the region of Oaxaca.

In addition to the ceremonial buildings, there are others where the governing class lived: the House of the Columns, the House of the Chultún (*cenote*), the House of the Halach Uinic, and others.

Other types of constructions, such as the rectangular and cruciform crypts inside some of the buildings, indicate an important cult of the dead. The population of Tulum seems to have been dedicated, in large part, to trade in specific products which they bartered with Central America and the Mexican Plateau.

The cove at one side of the Castillo must have been the place where the goods brought from zones such as Costa Rica and Panama or the eastern coast of the peninsula or the Gulf Coast of Mexico were unloaded. The products were honey — so important in the eastern coast of the peninsula that the Descending god has been interpreted as the representation of a bee—, wax, copal, fish, salt, quetzal feathers and objects in obsidian, as well as many others. Commerce was so important in the postclassic period on the Yucatán peninsula, and especially in some of its ports such as Tancáh and Tulum, that the paintings may display the distinct styles of the artists whom the rich merchants had brought here from far distant places.

Another structure which also has interesting paintings is the Temple of the Descending God, with a foundation of a single level which supports a small temple on the upper part, with the sloping walls typical of Tulum.

In the 19th century and during the War of Castes in Yucatán, Tulum served as a refuge for various rebellious groups of Maya Indians.

The Descending god, frequently depicted in Tulum, is related both to the planet Venus and to the setting Sun and also with the bee, whose honey the Mayas traded in.

Sea and earth form an arch which enhances the majesty of the monuments of Tulum.

CONTENTS

CREDITS

GIANNI DAGLI ORTI: Pages 4 left; 5; 6 right; 7; 8 above right; 8 below; 9 below; 10; 11; 12; 13; 14; 15 below right and left; 16; 26; 29 below; 30; 31; 32; 33; 36 below; 37; 44 below; 45; 50 above; 51 above; 59; 61 below; 68 above; 69; 70 above; 72; 73; 78; 86 above; 88; 92 above; 105 above; 112 above; 116; 122 above; 123.

ENRIQUE FRANCO TORRIJOS: Pages 4 right; 6 left; 8 above left; 9 above; 17 below; 91; 118; 119.

WALTER REUTER: Pages 51 below; 67 above; 104 below; 106; 121 above; 122 below; 126 above.

IRMGARD GROTH: Page 15 above.

JOSÉ DE LOS REYES M.: Page 17 above.

RUTH LECHUGA: Page 48 below.

JAS REUTER: Page 50 below.

Other photos belong to the archives of Bonechi Publishing House and were taken by Paolo Giambone.